Memoirs of a 'Lazy Korfa'

'TUNMISE USIKALU

Dearest Osi,

I hope you enjoy reading my book! There are 15 years between writing my journal in NYSC camp and eventually publishing the book. BE ENCOURAGED and always FOLLOW YOUR DREAMS!

WITH Love,

TUNMISE x

SOPHOS SB BOOKS

Memoirs of a 'Lazy Korfa'

Copyright © 2020 by Tunmise Usikalu

Published by
Sophos Books Ltd.
2 Woodberry Grove
London
N12 0DR

www.publishwithsophos.com

DISCLAIMER

The views portrayed in this journal are entirely that of the author and represent her view of actual events as they happened. This is not a complete historical account of all that happened during the NYSC orientation camp in Ungogo, Kano in September of 2004. Many of the characters have been written based on real people and real events. This journal did not seek for nor receive any endorsements from the *National Youth Service Corps*.

ISBN 978-1-905669-30-1

All rights reserved. No part of this publication may be reproduced, stored in a retrieval system, or transmitted in any form or by any means, mechanical, electronic, photocopying or otherwise without the prior written consent of the copyright owner.

Cover illustration and design by *Tolu Shofule*
Printed in the United Kingdom

To the Sweet Memory of my Sister,

MRS IWALOLA F. EMMANUEL

(Nee Awojobi)

10th January 1974 - 27th November 2001

You were not just my sister; you were also my friend. You made me feel like I could achieve anything I ever wanted. I still miss you terribly.

Continue to rest in peace my Sweetheart Sister,

till we meet again.

AND

To My Dad,

MR OLUYINKA A. AWOJOBI

9th April 1934 – 25th April 2007.

Even the littlest things made you proud.

This would have brought you much delight.

ACKNOWLEDGEMENTS

I cannot thank my family (the Awojobis & the Usikalus) and friends enough for all the love and support that have helped get this book out. There are not enough pages to name every single person so, as clichéd as this is, I'll just say you know who you are, so "Thank you from the bottom of my heart. Thank you for believing in me. Thank you so very much!"

Special thanks to the following people:

Theophilus Emmanuel, for giving me the final shove to keep a journal in camp since I "like writing so much."

Sisanmi Oma-Wilkie, for handing over her brand new exercise books just in time.

Seyi Adebayo-Olubi, for the initial ground work you did when we first thought to publish what was just my journal.

Bolaji Sofoluwe, for the fantastic plan that opened doors.

Sola Osinoiki, for the introduction and divine connections.

Tolu Shofule of *Imaginovation*, for the lovely cover illustration.

Modupe Adefeso-Olateju, Nnamdi Osuagwu, Yinka Awojobi, Adebola Williams, Chude Jideonwo and everyone else who supported this project in any way, big or small.

Tokunbo Emmanuel of *Sophos Books Ltd*, for taking the vision and running with it.

The lifelong friends I made while in Kano, my fellow 2004 Batch B Corp Members, the NYSC officials, Soldiers, Man O' War personnel and everyone else in camp without whom there would have been no journal.

My amazing husband and friend, Olumuyiwa, and our beautiful daughters; my world is so much better with you in it.

And to Jehovah, the One who gave everything to see me become great; I live for you now and always.

FOREWORD

The *National Youth Service Corps* (NYSC) has always been a scalpel of some sort, severing young people from the comfort of familiar surroundings and pushing them towards the unknown. In 2005, I graduated from the Nigerian Law School in Bwari and was posted to Lagos state to do the mandatory one-year programme. I was scared and happy at the same time; always accepting of a new adventure, but wondering how I would survive in this enclave of which I had heard various tales, many exaggerated, all nonetheless scary. NYSC, in "safe" Lagos, as it were, did live up to the hype of a new experience.

So, Tunmise's memories bring a smile to my face - running around for those early morning drills with waist pouches or "mobile central banks" as she calls them, with the cold stinging their backs; chanting those hilarious made-up-on-the-spot Man O' War songs that were the hallmark of spontaneity and raw ingenuity; evading soldiers and scampering away as they flung their whips with reckless abandon, happy to unleash them after seasons of little or no activity; the unbelievably low sanitary conditions of the Camp; the ubiquitous photographers and petty traders with more stamina than any Corper could boast of; of fresh love and love unrequited – as they remind me of similar experiences in my case. And then the people - the shock of people from across the country, forced to live together. It made for interesting perspectives of life.

Tunmise will agree. She was posted to Kano where she initially knew no one and had to adapt to a series of culture shocks and counter-cultures. In writing her memoirs, this young lady has documented her struggles and successes, as well as the highs and lows of the Service year. This book delves wholeheartedly into the world of a young woman who got a break she never even knew she needed; an introduction into the real world and to another side of Nigeria.

I haven't yet seen anyone document this literally-once-in-a-lifetime experience with humour, wit and simplicity as perfectly as she has done. In keeping a journal at the time and not waiting till she left Camp to pen down the sum total of happenings during her stay, she has done a generation's narrative an important favour. Her story is a refreshing one and will appeal to any new Corper about to enter into Camp as well as rake up nostalgic feelings for those who are done with it.

This generation doesn't document enough of its stories. For doing so, and doing it so well, I say thank you, Tunmise.

- Chude Jideonwo

Chief Executive Officer at, *Joy, Inc.* and Author of *Are We The Turning Point Generation?*

AUTHOR'S NOTE

Early in September of 2004, I proceeded to Kano State in Northern Nigeria to start my three-week stint at the National Youth Service Orientation camp in Ungogo. National Youth Service is a compulsory programme for Nigerian graduates that has been in place since 1973 to help foster national unity. Each graduate is "posted" to a State other than their State of origin for a year. They are expected to contribute to development in the area in one way or another, usually by teaching in local schools, working in Government Hospitals and Parastatals etc. in return for a salary paid to them by the Federal Government.

All members of the National Youth Service Corps (NYSC) are required to spend three weeks in an Orientation Camp at the beginning of their service year. This book started out as a journal I kept during my three weeks in Camp.

As you share in my Camp experience, I hope that those who have never had the opportunity to go to NYSC Camp would have an idea what it is like, and possibly conclude that they missed out on some good fun!

For those who have been to Camp, no matter how long ago, they will recall, perhaps with some nostalgia, their adventure. And to those who still have Camp ahead of them... well, now that you have a preview of what it is like, you can either look forward to it or be full of dread!

For everyone, as you follow my journey all the way to the last page, I hope you enjoy the reading experience, and gain something insightful, no matter how small - a word, a phrase, a joke, a lesson - just as I did.

DAY ONE
TUESDAY 070904

11:00 AM
DOMESTIC AIRPORT, LAGOS

I really should have started writing this last night but I was quite tired. I certainly feel a little more relaxed about the idea of going to Kano today than I have felt in the last few days.

It is 11:00am now, and I am still in the departure hall of the Murtala Muhammed domestic airport, waiting for the boarding call of an 11:15am flight. It does not even look as if they will be ready for us in another half hour as all other flights are also running late. All hail Nigeria!

I am not sure what to think or how I feel right now. I am trying hard to keep an open mind, but that is proving a bit difficult with all the horror stories I heard about the hard knock life of Camp. Anyway, I WILL SURVIVE! I do not have much of a choice, do I?

So funny how all the encouragement you give others — *Trust in God, Hope for the best* — flies out of the window when you need it. At the moment, I would rather not hear all the "God works in mysterious ways" gist that I so readily tell others!

Well, I hope it is not half as bad as I think, but I am not keeping my fingers crossed or holding my breath – better not to expect too much now!

Can all passengers for flight K223 flying to Kano, please proceed to the boarding gate…

Thank goodness!

2:30PM

Just arrived at Camp. It is really hot out here in Kano. I can only imagine what my complexion is going to look like at the end of three whole weeks!

On arrival at the Mallam Aminu Kano International Airport, I met three other girls going my way. Every other person, it seemed, was going to other states like Katsina, Jigawa, Yobe. Suddenly, I was at least grateful for not having to sit through another long journey in a car to get to Camp – it took us about fifteen minutes and N400 each. The four of us were checked at the gate and given some temporary identity cards.

Although this is only the first day of Camp, as at 2:30pm or thereabouts, I am already number One Thousand Two Hundred and Forty-Six! As if that is not bad enough, we get marched over to the registration hall to get registered and... wait for it... they are registering Corper number TWO HUNDRED AND SOMETHING! (I did not care to know what the 'something' was. It was not important).

So, here I am, sitting on my travelling bag under a tree for shade, wondering what in heaven's name I am doing here. Luckily for me, all pride aside, I had asked one of the cabin crew for an extra snack just before we landed, which he gave me – along with a drink for good measure. I am going to eat that now. I feel the hunger coming on...

7:00PM

At about 7:00pm, I heard a lady who was also sitting under a tree nearby, singing the hymn *It is well*. I smiled as I thought, "Poor lady, having to encourage herself!" I listened closely and realised she was singing along to a song she was playing on her Walkman. I listened more intently because the voice coming over the speakers sounded oddly familiar.

Alas, it was a familiar voice indeed. It was the voice of a friend and fellow choir member in my church in Lagos. She had done a rendition of *It is well* on our new album, *Friend of the Light*. That was what this Corper was playing in Kano,

Northern Nigeria. Well, the choir's vision was to declare God's praise to the "ends of the earth." That really did lighten up my evening as it was slowly starting to feel like a nightmare.

After sitting outside for almost 5 hours, we were informed that Camp officials have nothing to do with bed space allocation and we were to go in search of those ourselves. To think that I had been sitting under a tree and counting flies (okay, not that many actually) while some other girls were helping themselves to bed spaces and bunks in the hostels. *You must always ASK QUESTIONS!* Somehow, I do not seem to have learnt that particular lesson because it keeps coming back.

Needless to say, we barely got a space, never mind an entire bunk. After searching around for a while, I got the spring section of a bunk bed and laid it on the floor. Then, I spread my bed sheets and wrappers over it before lying down (almost directly on the floor, if you ask me).

After a short while, some girls started coming in with mattresses and they informed us that they had to exchange their call up letters for the semblance of comfort tonight. *Dangerous move*, I thought. *What if it becomes our turn to register and we don't have our call up letters with us?* What if this? What if that?

I laid on my makeshift bed for another thirty minutes and my need for comfort overtook what I thought was my better judgment. Jumping up, I took my call up letter to the store and promptly submitted it in exchange for a mattress. I slept much more comfortably than I could ever have done on the spring.

All well and good, as registration closed at about midnight and they were still at Corper number 600 or thereabout. Glad I listened to what turned out to be the better judgment after all!

DAY TWO
WEDNESDAY 080904

We had a little "incident" about 2:00am with some girls shouting, "Thief! Thief!" Not sure exactly what it was about, but security could be a whole lot better around here. We all have our "mobile central banks" around our waists in pouches. Our money goes with us everywhere. Who wants to be stranded in Kano?

Anyway, that disturbed my sleep a bit. But otherwise it was okay - not too cold; and the mosquito repellent I had bought last minute turned out to be a great help.

At 4:30am, the bugle sounded and we were asked to "fall out" for the morning drills, whether registered or not. People were wearing all sorts, including skirts and dresses. Even Muslim sisters had to do the morning drills in their full *hijab*! No one was exempt.

Initially, it was not so cold and I thought, "Not bad…" But for some crazy reason, the brighter it got, the colder it became!

It was annoying initially that they would ask us to come out for morning drills when we had not even done the most important thing–register! But it actually turned out all right, especially with the funny songs they made us sing while jogging. We jogged quite some distance, then did exercises before we were dismissed at about 7:30am and asked to return at 9:00am. We grumbled a bit as we returned to the hostels.

Now for the BIG ONE – bathing. Goodness! The make-shift bathrooms were small cubicles with walls made from aluminium roofing sheets and no roofs. They were located in the middle of the field between hostel blocks. As if that was not bad enough, there was such a long queue of girls. Well, there was another group that could not wait for the queues and probably could not be bothered. They were bathing in a space at the back of the last hostel block, which was "semi-secluded" but still somewhat open.

Well, yours truly did the unthinkable. I joined the brave bunch and did a ten second bath with twelve other girls on a row! If they had told me I would be doing such a thing, I would have said "impossicant" (that is, it cannot be possible)! But you see, by that time, I had switched off completely. I had a culture shock last night and as I sat on my "bed," I was so fed up. I just did not seem to care any longer.

The rest of the day was spent *trying* to register.

The mother of all rains fell at about 6:30pm and it was so cold!

DAY THREE
THURSDAY 090904

We had to get up at 4:00am for the early morning drill. It was so terribly cold. Thank God I thought to bring a cardigan as I needed one this morning. I think it is crazy that they would wake us up at 4:00am, drive us to the parade ground like cattle, and make us stand there till about 6:00am or so when it is bright enough to go jogging outside the school where we were based. We just stood there as they went on cracking all sorts of jokes. It got really annoying but they seemed to believe it taught us something (I'm still trying to figure out what!). It was kind of fun, although the initial getting up was really annoying.

The *Man O' War* guys in charge of the morning drills only ever spoke in broken English, which made everything they said doubly funny. Whenever they see Corpers squatting, they would say stuff like, "Dem say make you send your first born come you say na you wan come." I found that hilarious. They also regularly said, "I wan serve, I wan serve. Oya serve now!" Of course, needless to say, they also cracked some not-too-clean jokes, which is not strange, all things considered!

Anyway, I had to continue with my registration today and I was so frustrated with it all! We can be so backward in Nigeria sometimes; it almost makes you stand in awe. It does not make things better the way the Corpers bring their university unruliness to Camp and shunt queues. I would stand in line and be on the same spot for about 30 minutes (no exaggeration), because several guys and girls could not be bothered to be as decent and orderly as others. These people just kept going straight to the front to beg or even claim some imaginary position. At the end of the day the aerial view of the queue looked something like this:

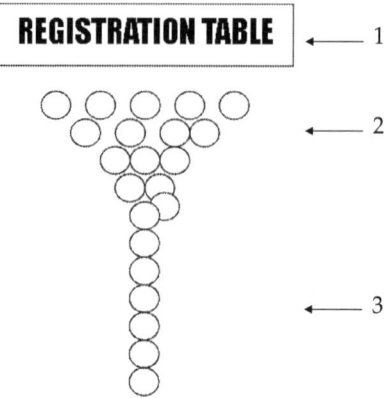

1. The Camp officials were, I presume, really frustrated with the heat and noise. They seemed to have really short fuses, constantly getting angry and storming out of the unbearably hot registration hall at every chance!
2. The "queue shunters" who felt the rest of us have come to sell groundnut in Kano and did not want to register.
3. The people who seemed to have nothing better to do than to stand on the same spot in a queue for hours on end, being taken for granted by the people in Group 2.

Anyway, I was just too tired to even struggle with anyone. I was tired from suddenly having to wake up two or more hours earlier than I usually do, doing some jogging and then doing several exercises. Not wanting to struggle did cost me, but I could not be bothered.

To make matters worse, it was not just one point for registration. We had to go through this harrowing experience about eight times because they had split the process into eight steps. We needed to fill different bits of information at each step. There was one queue for State of origin, another for university, another for the course you studied and two for allowances. The queues for allowances were the longest and most disorderly ones (apart from the queue for the call-up register).

At about 5:00pm, the officials had a sudden wave of not-so-common sense, as one Corper put it. We were split into about five groups, according to our numbers, and life became a whole lot better afterwards. The shunting and disorderliness reduced drastically since at each point we were being attended to according to our numbers. If this registration process had been thought through from the start, this is probably how we would have been attended to from the beginning. Sometimes, we prefer the more difficult approach to work in Naija, because that way, we can feel like we have actually done something. Lord have mercy!

By the time it was 10:00pm, I had finished all I needed to do and just had my kit to collect. The State Director had promised that whatever happened we would all leave Camp with our complete kit. There were no promises about how long you would get to wear it in Camp for though! We had been reliably informed that the Corpers in Camp were actually about twice the number they had initially anticipated, so you can imagine there was some shortage by this time and we started hearing there were no more belts, caps and crested vests. Corpers collecting their kits late had to come back later to queue AGAIN for these when they became available.

On a much brighter note, what joy today when I 'discovered' Chizoba Ugwu - a familiar face at last! I suddenly felt much better because it was odd trying to flow with some of the people I was stuck with. Okay, not really 'stuck', but a familiar face is always welcome. Although, it is funny how your ability to bond with complete strangers quadruples when you are thrown together in adverse conditions.

I have known Chizzy for as long as I can remember. We grew up in the same area. I did not know we had been posted to the same place until I ran into him at the mammy market today. We lost contact when they moved away, but I knew he was studying Architecture. He had actually been around since early on Tuesday, but we just found each other – the Camp was big.

We quickly caught up on old times and I asked about everyone — his parents, his brothers and even those cousins of his who did not seem to leave their house in those days. We exchanged phone numbers and he promised to call me later in the day.

I went to the clinic to register and found there were actually Doctors and other Medical personnel staying in the building permanently. Well, what do you know? The advantages of being a Doctor in this place are numerous. No one actually really disturbs you for anything like they do the others.

We did not have to attend the morning drills, the logic being if we do, who gets to treat the injured when they start trooping in? The soldiers do not come into the clinic to chase anyone out. The most they do is come in, crack a few jokes, be sure no one was hiding out here and leave – RESPECT! The six-plus-x years I spent studying Dentistry are starting to pay dividends.

I have been placed on several days of call during the three weeks of Camp. The call entails being permanently in the clinic during the period assigned, which was fine by me because I did not have to go to the parade ground to march under the scorching heat of Kano's mid-day sun!

I went back to collect my kit later. The evil spirit of unruliness came upon its own again at about 10:00pm and they proceeded to completely disrupt the queue for kit collection, which made the Camp officials really angry. They left at about 10:30pm, although they had initially promised to be there till midnight. Just as well, I thought. Who wants to collect half a kit and then queue again to collect the other half? I was even too stressed from all the standing and moving from one unprogressive queue to the next and back again. What made the queuing even more disorderly was that one person would have spaces on all queues and just as you behold the table so close to you, some five or so people can just fix themselves ahead of you claiming to be "behind her" or "in front of him."

Some people allowed them into the queue without protesting, while others were up in arms and some even got physical. This happened when everyone still had some energy. By the time we were all really tired of standing, once you were not on the queue for longer than 5-10 minutes, you would be hard pressed to find anyone who would allow you back in the queue.

In short, I did not collect my kit and went to bed, still feeling somewhat satisfied that, at least, I was at the very end of registration - a gruesome and harrowing experience!

While on the queue, a guy had said there is no reason why NYSC could not have asked for the details of our outfits and shoe sizes at the same time that our names were sent to them for our posting. This could have helped to reduce the problem of oversized and undersized kits. I agreed that it was possible if we put our hearts to it.

For instance, there was a section in one of the forms we filled that asked for our statistics, like shirt size, trouser length, shoe size etc. Even with all that, a lot of us still got at least two sizes above our shoe size and three to four sizes above our clothes sizes. We ended up having to spend an extra N200 amending the outfit so it did not look like a carpenter built the NYSC kit! It would make sense to send in the statistics form for the final year students at universities to fill out. The universities will then return these to them along with the list of people whose names are sent for mobilisation. That way, as they do the postings, they also have a general idea of the sizes that would be needed in each camp based on the statistics of the people being sent there. I dare say they could even go as far as preparing each person's kit that would be personalised so that as you report and register you just pick up your own kit with all the right sizes.

I dream...

DAY FOUR
FRIDAY 100904

On the food tip, quickly. So far, I have been surviving on corn flakes in the morning and rice in the afternoon, plus lots of water (because of the heat). I have not yet been able to psych myself enough to eat the food we are being given. Maybe it is because I still have money.

There are a good number of food joints at the Mammy Market, and being the unadventurous person that I am, I have just picked one and stuck with it; and I eat only rice! Yesterday, however, Mr. Bigg's opened a stand in Camp and one of the times that I was really frustrated with the "non-moving" queue, I decided to treat myself to Fried Rice and Chicken. (I hope I wont 'pay' for it later).

I had now become humble and decided to collect the incomplete kit, instead of insisting on not wanting to queue twice. Right now, even the Camp officials didn't know when the rest of the kit would be available. Half bread, they say, is better than none. My plan was to go straight to the store early in the morning to collect whatever I could of the kit. When the soldiers blew their whistles and blasted that irritating sound of the bugle at 4:00am, I got up and walked straight to the Clinic. I went to look for my new Pharmacist friend, Linda. I lay beside her on her mattress and set my alarm for about 6:30am and tried to get a little extra sleep. In the distance, I could hear the soldiers shouting orders and chasing the rest of the girls out of their rooms, while the Medics in the Clinic just snored away except for one or two that actually wanted to go for the morning drill.

I can already tell the difference between the last 3 days and today, the extra two hours or so of sleep has made me feel a lot less cranky than I have felt in the last 72 hours.

By the time I got to the store, I was number 30 on the queue — at 7:00 am in the morning! Of course, we didn't all go for the drill. Where there is a will, there is a way. Speaking of which, these solders must get a special kind of high from driving us out of the rooms and seeing us scamper around.

Once, a male soldier came to send us out for parade at about 9:00am, right after breakfast. One girl shouted, "Don't come in, we are naked o!" For some reason, the soldier was infuriated by that statement and went on about how the male and female soldiers in the camp were all staying in the same room. He then said, "Na breast I never see before? Stupid girl." The soldier went on and on and on.

I found it very interesting that the statement would get such a reaction and was wondering if there was a problem between him and the girl that we knew nothing of. I could not get over the disproportionate reaction. I later found out the guy just has a very short fuse!

Anyway, I collected my kit in no time and concluded that the demons of unruliness and theirs were either on the field or still asleep. I got size 7 boots. I could not believe my luck because hardly anyone I knew got boots in their size and people had to go around exchanging.

But that's where the good news ends. I got the "smallest" available size of canvas, size 9, a good two sizes above what I wear. All the tissue I brought to camp will finally be put to use. The khakis were like my Dad's "agbada" and "shokoto" on me - big and long. Of course, there were lots of standby tailors near the store to help adjust them at a price.

I shut my eyes and wore them like that. After all, Camp is not a fashion show and if it is, I could not be bothered. I did not wear the khakis. I wore my white shorts and shirt instead along with my tissue-padded size 9 canvas on my size 7 feet. How could I have forgotten just how tight the socks were? Designed to completely cut off all blood supply!

4:00PM

I had a very interesting experience today. We were asked to go for a lecture on HIV/AIDS, but I did not want to go and "roast" in the hall. It is so hot in that place and ventilation was poor. So, I went to the Mr. Bigg's stand located in one of the classrooms to have a snack. I joined a lady who was sitting alone on a table and began to write.

The lady then started asking me my name, what university I went to etc. I told her my profession and like everyone I tell, she had a question to ask. She wanted to know about dentures. I explained to her what they were. She then wanted to know if it had any effects on the health of a wearer. I answered her. I thought it was odd the way she was so interested but didn't ask her why. Well, I didn't need to because before I knew it, she told me all I wanted to know and more.

She is so crazy about good dentition and it rates very high on her "husband must have" list. It was difficult for her when she found out her new boyfriend wears dentures because she thought, "How could God do this to me?" It wasn't just about the dentures actually; the dentures were the climax. He generally did not have a very good set of teeth and unlike all the other people she'd ever dated, she wanted God to confirm over and over again to her that he was the one (of course, she got her confirmation).

There was something she said that really impressed me. She said as much as she desired for her man to have good dentition, she realised that there was something he had she could never trade for good dentition. "My baby is a beautiful person right from inside." I could see the sincerity of those words in her eyes. She just went on and on about how he's got character and he is a good person not just to her, but also to others. I was really impressed.

So, I sat there listening and I just knew that I wasn't meant to be at that HIV/AIDS lecture. I was supposed to be with her at that time, at that place. I let her know that I agreed with her; that some things are certainly more important than others. I put my Dentist hat on and let her know all hope is not lost; that there were several things that can be done to completely transform his dentition. I also told her that if it mattered to her that much, she should discuss it with him, and they can both work at making his dentition better, which would help her become more comfortable with and confident in her man.

It was a very fulfilling thirty minutes or so. She even took my number so they could call me later. I felt really good after talking with her and realised that there will always be opportunities to encourage people along the way. She is a Christian and her fiancé also. She said her Pastor teased her by saying, "God don catch you!" It's amazing how God will sometimes just take a good look at you and ask you to let go of that thing you cherish so much and it will initially seem like you'll die without it, but you always are better for it.

The rest of the day was pretty uneventful except for a terrible sand storm and rain that fell late in the evening. We all ended up sleeping early which was all well and good, really.

DAY FIVE
SATURDAY 110904

I got up at the same odd hour of 4:00am and decided to go to the parade ground. We were divided into platoons yesterday and we jogged in our platoons today. We went out of the gate for the first time and jogged quite a distance. Of course, we were quite a spectacle for the people in the neighbourhood and they all came onto the road to stare.

We now have platoon leaders who were democratically elected yesterday. Initially, our platoon instructor picked three guys and three girls and asked us to vote (for one guy as leader and a girl as assistant), but it didn't quite work out. The instructor then decided to write on three small pieces of paper and ask them to pick. Of course (as always), it was the guy who looked least interested that picked the winning paper. His name is Toyosi. He looked a little reserved, like butter would not melt in his mouth!

Well that was yesterday. Today, Toyosi seems to have entered into the spirit of being a platoon leader because he is shouting out marching instructions.

People are desperately trying to find a way out of NYSC. As for me, I wanted to do NYSC, but Kano? It is so hard for me to accept, but also it cannot be so easy to leave when you are in such an "obvious" profession and you are practically the only one in the entire batch of Corpers! I cannot even think of what would make me stay. Right now, I just want to see where I will get posted to first – maybe, just maybe, I may be convinced...

2:30PM

I called a friend of mine to ask where I will likely be posted. She had just finished from Kano and was also in my peculiar discipline. She thought I would definitely be within town. If that were to be so, I don't know yet if I would be happy or sad. Well, happy because I'll be within civilisation; sad, perhaps, because this is where the fighting and crisis usually starts from when they happen. So I was told. As they say: safety first.

I have to admit, I'm actually starting to give in a bit to the idea of staying in Kano, but I am just not at all comfortable with the entire crisis situation I have heard of in the past. It is interesting how what you hear can completely make or mar something (or someone) even before it starts.

Anyway, I am also a bit encouraged by the book I am reading right now – *The Purpose-driven Life*. It speaks extensively of God being pleased when His people trust Him to keep His promises, help with our problems and do the impossible, when necessary. But I am also quick to admit that God is so multifaceted and sovereign that He is still at liberty to do (or allow) whatever and it will not change who He is. That is scary, really scary; because you can't go around acting like God owes you.

4:00PM

I went for afternoon drills. Then we had games and sports - football for guys and volleyball for girls. There was also the drama and dance group for those who were interested. Naturally, I decided to join that group.

There is a drama and dance competition between all the platoons being organised for next week. We have very little time to come up with something and rehearse since our presentation is on Monday night. We had rehearsals right after the games and sports so we could put something together. Our platoon instructor seems to be a sore loser and since he won the drama competition at the previous orientation camp, he has a reputation to protect.

It is so difficult to get people from different

backgrounds to put a drama together under 48 hours, but with a bit of tolerance and maturity from everyone, I think it is possible...

As things would turn out, the drama meeting was so much fun. I also got myself a part; although I am yet to understand what it is about, but just having a part in the play will do for now.

Nigerian Breweries organised a welcome night for the Corpers tonight, with free drinks at the Mammy Market.

When I got back to my room after drama rehearsals, I heard something I thought was sad in some regard. Some guy brought a camcorder to camp and was filming stuff. He had just left my room and had shown the girls in the room shots of a girl who had gotten herself drunk at the welcome party and was really misbehaving. In the video, there was a guy dragging her off somewhere, both of them with beer bottles in hand. I don't want to imagine where that girl might wind up tonight. It is strange that even with all the State Director's warnings, people would still go ahead and jeopardise their lives in the name of fun. The State Director had spoken extensively about how some people "meet their waterloo" in Camp and get infected with HIV/AIDS. We all thought he was exaggerating, but after a few days of being here alone, I can see that he was only talking from experience.

Speaking of people jeopardising their lives, there is this lady in my platoon who is so pregnant even a blind man can see it. But she tries to hide the pregnancy and attends drills like everyone else. I cannot understand why she would risk losing her baby or getting some horrible infection from the poor hygiene conditions around here.

Well, someone argued that a pregnant woman in this batch will be a nursing mother the next batch; and a nursing mother next batch can be pregnant again before the batch after that. As none of them are allowed legally in the orientation camp, she might as well. True, but I am still not so sure about the wisdom in it!

DAY SIX
SUNDAY 120904

Today I went for the *Nigerian Christian Corpers' Fellowship (NCCF)* meeting for the first time. The Preacher spoke on "Fulfilling God's Will in Marriage." Well, it is a valid topic, because I hear people, a lot of people, meet their spouses during the NYSC year. I've even heard that it is encouraged and an award or money is given to them by NYSC! All this to foster national unity and integration… so they say!

4:00PM

More drama rehearsals today. I joined the NCCF drama unit as well after service, but ended up missing the rehearsal later in the day because I overslept!

It is really hard to fathom when people come out of the blue and feel they can make last minute changes to the drama. Why were they not there yesterday to make suggestions? Anyway, that's their problem; I just want to do my best and contribute to the overall success of the platoon.

Meanwhile I still have not worn my Khaki because I am hoping they will look kind of new when I take my official NYSC picture in my crested vest (when I finally get it!).

7:30PM

We just started rehearsing the "new" drama tonight. I cannot seem to hide. They always seem to find me a part to play even if it means making one up. Anyway, a city set on a hill cannot be hidden, I suppose.

The soldiers are making noise again, wanting us to go to bed. Lights out, so got to go soon! Meanwhile, it is raining heavily and getting really cold. Something tells me morning drills tomorrow would not be pleasant. Luckily for us, we have not all been kitted so I can still wear my jeans and not get harassed. Can very easily catch a cold (maybe even pneumonia) in this Camp! The officials and soldiers cannot tell who has been given a complete kit and who hasn't. This means we are all still not strictly wearing our khakis which is great!

Today was even worse because a lot of the girls dressed up in *geles* and wrappers for service. I, on the other hand, was quite happy to wear my jeans and white T-shirt. One of my friends could not go for her own service because they said trousers were not allowed. Is that *really* necessary?

DAY SEVEN
MONDAY 130904

Right after morning drills, the drama group did not go out jogging with the rest of the platoon as today is our drama presentation day. We were in a mess really because we had started another new drama last night at our instructor's command. But who are we to protest? Here, we are expected to follow the last command and not do any thinking.

We rehearsed almost through the morning, and were to meet again in the evening. I later heard the crested vest, caps and belts were ready for collection from the store for those of us with incomplete kits. This was at about 3:00pm. Well, needless to say, I was out for another queuing nightmare, which did not end till five hours later. I got my crested vest around 8:00pm, fondly referred to as 'Christmas dress' by the soldiers.

I was very tired and frustrated. I had missed the rehearsals and actually was willing to give up the role if need be because I felt it was more important to collect my Christmas dress! My role was minor and could be dumped if need be.

The drama was about a Hausa guy who had met an Igbo girl in camp and fallen in love with her. He then asked her to marry him. As expected, both sets of parents refused at first, but later agreed to "One Nigeria."

Well, believe it or not, the other platoon presenting their drama that night had the same story line—Igbo girl, Hausa boy, vexed parents vexing—and they presented theirs before us! But what did it for us was our costuming and make-up. We had contributed N200 each in the platoon and gone to the market to buy what we needed. It was lovely and we were obviously the better team. We took lots of pictures afterwards, and I hope my face showed in them!

It is not so cold tonight, although it drizzled a bit.

DAY EIGHT
TUESDAY 140904

At last, I have learnt my lesson. I no longer jump out at the first sound of the bugle and end up standing on the parade ground for an hour before anything starts. Today, I got up after about 20 minutes, changed and lay down on my bed again, while the soldiers were making noise outside. I soon realised that like me, there were many girls still in the room.

Some of the girls were actually doing "fine art" at 5 O' clock in the morning. Why would you want to put on make up at this time? Who exactly is worth the trouble in Camp? Man O' war guys or Corpers?

It is hard to keep up with all the slangs that the soldiers use. When Corpers start acting tired or we do not do the drills correctly, the soldiers call us "Otondo" Corpers. I think it is another name for dummies or something. And the songs they make us sing when jogging are so funny! One of the songs we sing goes:

Comot for road O
Comot for road
Lazy corper comot for road

Well, being in the North, what we heard the soldiers (some of them, at least) sing was "Lazy KORFA". Initially, we all used to sing "Lazy Corper," but not for long. Now, mimicking the soldiers, everyone sings "Lazy Korfa." It's hilarious!

When the soldiers came back at 9:00am to get us back to the field, I went to the clinic instead. Goodness, don't these soldiers ever get tired? They must get a kick from it all really.

After everyone went over to the field, I left the clinic and went to take a picture in my "Christmas dress." I hope it turns out nice because that picture in the crested vest is *the* iconic NYSC picture!

Our platoon instructor changed the platoon leader today to another guy. I think it was a good choice. The new guy looks like he will make a good leader. Toyosi does not seem like he's hurt about being dethroned anyway. We talked a bit today.

I also saw Chizzy this morning. He is in another platoon. I have been seeing him around with this girl and I'm wondering, what's up? I seem to recall that he mentioned a girlfriend to me when we were catching up. Hmmm… I shall be asking questions most definitely!

How could I have forgotten the comedy moment we had after drills. Our volleyball team played against another platoon's team. It was terrible. They were so bad someone asked, "Is this the real thing or are they practising?"

The girls were such a joke. Towards the end, we started shouting that their boys should please join in the game; that we would not mind! The game was over in less than 30 minutes. It was that terrible. I suppose it did not help that our girls wore nice jerseys and they didn't; and that our supporters were very loud and theirs were not. It was so bad it felt like they came to sell groundnut in Kano!

8.00PM

My good friend, Toks, came to do some work in Kano and dropped by to see me at the Camp. It was really good to see him. In his usual manner, he had loads of encouragement to give. He spoke a lot on focusing on the vision, and revisiting it if it appears to have blurred out a bit.

I like to see Toks and talk with him. He is such an inspiration. But seeing him sometimes makes me feel guilty because I'm reminded that there is still so much for me to do! Anyway, I pray God's will be done over all else, ultimately.

Off to bed now!

DAY NINE
WEDNESDAY 150904

Today was my "off-day." I went straight to the clinic after the morning drills to report sick and get a sick report for two days. My back was starting to kill me and my whole body was aching. So, I pretty much lay on my bed all day except for when I had my bath and went to eat.

Something interesting happened at morning drill. One of the Muslim sisters refused to obey the last command and got our instructor really angry! He had been teaching us to "slow march" and showed us a trick which was meant to help us remain in a straight line when doing the slow march. He asked us to hold each other discreetly with our little fingers, while marching very close together, shoulder to shoulder. Of course, the sister refused to do that because she was between two brothers.

That vexed our instructor and was enough to make him spit some early morning fire. I, for once, kind of agreed with him, because it seemed a little bit unnecessary as she was not the only Muslim sister there at the time, and everyone else said nothing about it.

Anyway, our instructor had to eventually give in to her and place her between two female Corpers instead. It seems to me like they are given preferential treatment, which does not go down well with everyone else. This creates a divide and an atmosphere that promotes favouritism. I don't know what can be done, but it sometimes leaves a bad taste in the mouth.

Because I was feeling quite sick today, Chizzy came to see me with his new friend, Ebere. She says she has a diagnosis for me – love sickness! Now, I don't know about that.

Chizzy came back on his own later in the day and I promptly asked him how far. "She's just a friend, it's nothing," he had said. I am weary of those kind of things and I was quick to tell him, especially when they spend so much time together in this enclosed space called Camp.

Not much happened for the rest of the day.

DAY TEN
THURSDAY 160904

I did not go for morning drill today and had my sick report in hand to show any solider that came in to chase us out. Some of them act like they are high on something. I am convinced they also get a kick from seeing us scamper around.

My roommates are getting increasingly daring, though. There were so many of us that did not go to the parade ground this morning and only two of us had sick reports to show. The rest have obviously grown wings!

The soldiers did come back at about 7:00am to chase girls out. They asked all the people they met sleeping to get down and carry their mattresses on their heads. My roommates dived under the bed; that is, they created spaces under beds where there were none previously! Speaking of which, the beds in my room have all been reconstructed using strips of the khaki material left following all the adjustments most people had done to their khakis. All the bunk beds have at least one corner tied in place with khaki because a lot of the metal holders at the corners were missing. The beds in my row are all tied together to give them more support, so if one comes down…

We were told Uncle Walter Oki (as we referred to the Director-General of NYSC) was coming and we had to report in our full kit to the parade ground at about 9:00am. The full kit is also called 7/7 by the soldiers (that is all seven pieces of the kit) including the khaki shirt in this scorching sun! Well, we are government property and as I said before, we are not supposed to think; our 'bosses' do the thinking for us and we just obey the last command!

I decided to get off my lazy backside and go see Uncle Walter. I had my bath and went to the clinic to meet Linda. Then we headed to the parade ground just as some Corpers were returning! (Honestly, Linda is bad for me and my efforts at being a good corps member). By the time we got to the field, we just managed to join the tail end of the marching as the last remaining Corpers left the field! Uncle Walter was still on his way and they said they will sound the bugle for us to gather again as soon as he was near enough.

We had our cultural dance rehearsal, so I left Linda and went for that. At the end of rehearsal on the way to my room, minding my own business, a guy walked up to me. I would not normally entertain this but I recognised him. I think he has a friend in my platoon that he goes everywhere with.

He introduced himself as Akan, said he had been watching me for some time now (jobless?) and he would like to be my friend. Well, I actually think it is quite a compliment for someone (not just anyone, though) to see you and just want to be your friend because they feel you've got something to offer.

Akan did not look like a riff raff. He is from Cross River but has lived in Lagos all his life and speaks Yoruba so fluently he would pass for a Yoruba guy. He studied Theatre Arts and also liked Karate (Help!). He said I looked quiet and not quiet at the same time. Of course, I quickly realised that like the other lady, there was certainly a reason for this because he proceeded to really talk to me as we slowly walked towards my room. Sometimes, I wonder if I have a poster on my head that says, "You can confide in me; talk to me." But I am happy about it because I do want to be an encouragement to people around me in any way possible.

We talked for a while and then went our separate ways. He told me he had a girlfriend back in Lagos and that made me happy for some strange reason. It will be really terrible for someone to go back on their commitment in three weeks of being here. However, it does seem some of us just allow boredom get the better of us. Then again…

The Director-General, Uncle Walter Oki, finally came at about 4:00pm and he stayed all of 20 minutes. He was very informal and sounded like a really nice man. He also sang his version of Fela's song, *Water no get enemy*. He sang, "Oki O l'ota O, Walter he no get enemy." It was very funny, though some people were sure he was only trying to console himself! He gave us N150,000 which made all the Corpers scream and clap. That was before they calculated how much it came to per head — about N75 each, assuming the money does not develop wings! Ha! Ha!

I hung out with Chizzy and of course, by extension, Ebere, since they seem to go everywhere together now. I spoke with her at length. She did not go to university in Nigeria. She studied one of those exotic-sounding courses that I cannot remember now, but it is in the management line, I think. She came back to the country about two years ago and has worked since then. She suddenly realised she may not be able to dodge NYSC for long as she has got big political plans (why ever?). So, according to her, she decided to just get it out of the way. Really nice girl. She is also fun to be with. Hmmm… Chizzy…

I got a call from a guy called Mohammed, a very posh Hausa guy. I met him on the queue while waiting to collect my crested vest. We gisted about Nigeria and about the developed world. He is very well-travelled and runs a Non-Governmental Organisation (NGO). He's certainly much older than most people in this batch if you ask me. He wanted to know where I was. I had no interest in hanging out with him at this time of night, so I promptly told him I was in my room getting ready for bed.

Good night!

DAY ELEVEN
FRIDAY 170904

Woke up today feeling really blue. I intended to go to the parade ground for the morning drill but ended up not going. It is that time of the month and I am in no mood to wear white shorts. I looked for my life-saving sick report in my pouch and held it to show any soldier that came along this morning. They did come as usual, but decided not to come into the room. They made all their entire noise outside today.

I took my bath very early before the others got back from drills and went to the clinic to see Linda.

There was a mini-drama in the afternoon. When it was time to go to the parade ground, we were in the clinic when we heard lots of noise just outside. "According to" (like my Aunt would say), we heard that the soldiers caught two guys and two girls in one of the hostels "playing rough." I do not know how true it is, but "according to," that's what caused the trouble.

The soldiers started chasing everyone out of the hostels and were really angry. They did not listen to anyone. One particular girl, who had a swollen leg from a previous injury, was carrying water. A soldier accosted her and asked her to go to the parade ground. While she was trying to explain, he is said to have taken the water from her, poured it over her and even stepped on her foot, leaving a wound on her little toe.

That was unreasonable if you ask me, but as if the girl had been itching for a chance like that, she began to display like a drama queen. She cried and wailed and rolled on the dirty, dusty floor. She refused to be pacified and refused for any doctor to touch her. Finally, she got the attention of the Camp commandant, Camp director and other officials. She was terribly rude to them and did not seem to care much. I thought she overreacted or perhaps it was just all that accumulated stress.

The most embarrassing thing, however, was that after all the high drama, when she finally allowed the medics to treat her, the Camp director asked her, "So what do you want us to do for you now?" She said she will not agree to anything until they buy her... wait for it... A bottle of Maltina! Goodness, gracious me! You mean all that noise ended with a N70 bottle of malt drink? The girls were all so embarrassed!

Well, the Camp director had to get her the Maltina and she finally cooled down. Of course, the Camp director could not let it pass; he spoke about it again and again as he could not get over it, and neither could we!

Meanwhile, outside the clinic, the other Corpers used the opportunity to lay about and not go where they were asked to go. They were exchanging words with soldiers and almost starting an *Aluta*! Some action at last. I am not surprised, though, because in the last few days, it has been building up with little eruptions here and there.

Later in the day, we had our first football match in my platoon. I like my platoon. We don't know how to march or do all that fancy parade stuff, but when it comes to drama, volleyball and football, we always do so well. Surely, that is enough!

I saw Akan on the parade ground and he asked me to go with him for NCCF after the football match. I really didn't want to go (I had only been for the Sunday morning meeting since I came). I have to admit, I was probably too scared what I would hear from the radical ministers they had coming for the meetings.

Eventually, I agreed to go with him. I got to NCCF at about 7:00pm and the meeting was actually nice. We had a preacher talk on "I must work the works of Him who sent me." For once,

Memoirs of a 'Lazy Korfa' 57

someone told us the truth. He said that a lot of what we had heard about Kano before coming was probably true. Everyone else said they were all lies. But he encouraged us that those who know their God will be strong and do exploits. He said he ran for about six hours non-stop during the last crisis! Yikes! You sure have to know who sent you to Kano: NYSC, FG or God!

During the testimony time, there were songs and testimonies. Akan did a recital. It was really good. We are definitely alike in some respect and I imagine he is a friend worth having. Also during testimonies, another Corper told of God's goodness. As she and some other Corpers from *Enugu State University of Technology* were coming to Camp, their driver and some passengers had connived to rob them in the bus. It was apparently very bad because she just found herself in the hospital. She had been unconscious. She said a girl was raped and a guy was badly beaten. It was really terrible, but God was merciful to her. Another reason to thank God for big and small mercies!

After fellowship, Akan and I went to eat. For some strange reason, I decided to show him the text messages on my phone. I cannot remember what we were talking about that led to it... Okay, I was asking about his girlfriend and if they were in touch – trying to play it safe. He is a good guy from the little I know but...

We went toward my room after dinner, stopped to gist with a mutual friend along the way, and then I went to my room.

Meanwhile, more and more people are leaving camp. Chizzy had arranged to spend the weekend out with some friends, but it did not work out. He had packed his stuff and mentally switched off from Camp for the weekend. Needless to say, he was very disappointed he did not get to go. Ebere, on the other hand, seemed very happy about his bad luck. She is not hiding the fact that she likes him at all!

Chizzy also says stupid things like she has "gotten into his system." I have been sounding the alarm bells from the start, but the boredom of Camp has made them spend more time together than they probably would have on a good day. Talking about their respective boyfriend/girlfriend is not working either, it appears.

I have told Chizzy it might be safest to run (I am not one to hang around and find stuff out!). But run to where exactly? This Camp is like a tiny shoebox! Anyway, I have made myself the self-appointed chaperone and will continue to nag him! Ebere is also a very good looking girl. I would vote her amongst the top three finest in Camp (I kid you not!). So, I think it also trips Chizzy that she had picked him out of everyone else. The stupid boy!

DAY TWELVE
SATURDAY 180904

The soldiers came in like a mighty rushing wind this morning. Instead of their usual two to each hostel block they came in droves like, twenty of them or something. They made so much noise, banging on windows and doors with sticks. It was scary. They were blowing whistles and shouting. It was like something out of a movie.

Anyway, I got out as soon as the mob came because they seemed a bit "higher" than usual, probably from all that drama with the girl yesterday. By the time they got to the block after mine, the girls came out, gathered together and started singing for them:

Na who go tire?

Soja go tire!

How many sojas Corper go beat O?

Eeeee we go beat dem tire!

You can just imagine the chaos at 4:30am in the morning! I had a good laugh, but was silently praying it would not get out of hand as tempers were rising and everyone seemed so angry, "Korfas" and "sojas" alike!

By the time drills started, there was a little drama between the two soldiers in charge of my platoon. In front of the whole platoon? How are we supposed to respect them if they cannot show themselves respect? Some people said the younger guy must have godfathers in the army otherwise he would not have dared to be so rude to his senior in rank. But then, maybe he was just high on something...

I finished from the field, had a bath and had to return for 9:00am. I got back there late and I think they may have chosen the people who will march already. They chose the first fifty in each platoon and asked the rest of us to stay on the side lines and cheer them while they marched. I certainly did not mind. I was just listening to music with my Walkman and dancing. Someone looked at me and said, "You are always in a world of your own; always reading or writing." I am not sure if that was a compliment.

We had a clinical presentation by a pharmaceutical company today. We had one by a different company yesterday. There is no getting away from this academic stuff is there? Even in Camp, we are still having seminars! I have chosen this path now, but maybe in my next life...

Chizzy saw me writing in my journal today and started teasing me about making my journal entries correctly. He said he hopes I am writing EVERYTHING in it. Well, as far as I can tell, I am. I think he may have been referring to Akan...

DAY THIRTEEN
SUNDAY 190904

I was at fellowship this morning. It went okay. The rest of the day was spent with Chizzy and Ebere, mostly. Chizzy is getting really bold with this undying love he is professing and I just cannot get over it. I think it may be more serious than I first thought.

I have spoken to Chizzy and all he has to say is that he really, likes her but will wait until he leaves Camp before he knows exactly how he feels. Ebere has invited us over for lunch when we get back home. Chizzy is not too sure about that as he does not want his girlfriend getting wind of this at all (she would not be amused). I think Ebere's fella is not even in the country, so that is not a problem for her.

The rest of the day was so dry except for when I saw Akan sometime in the afternoon. He came to the clinic to see a Doctor. He asked me to escort him to lunch so he could take his medication and I did. He asked if I had any new text messages since the ones I showed him. I told him none that I would want him to see, which really meant none at all.

Later, it was Drama Night at NCCF, and I had opted out of acting. So, I went to watch. Akan was there as well.

I still cannot get over how people can "fall in love" within three weeks of Camp, but I suppose anything is possible! Anyway, if you can "fall in love" with someone in this place, where people cannot afford to look their best (though some people defy the odds) then it might be you like the person's company or something else besides looks, I THINK!

Speaking of looking your best, some people brought so many outfits; they even brought *geles* to Camp. If you see some people on Sunday morning, you would think they left for the NCCF meeting straight from their own houses. I find it pretty amusing!

Anyway, back to Akan who said he would like me to pray that his prayers would be answered. "What prayers?" I asked. "That I would not fall for *you* before this Camp is over," was his answer.

Right. See trouble!

Anyway, his relationship did not sound like a steady one. As far as I knew, he had spoken with her just twice since we came. I could not imagine that! It would probably be easy to fall for someone else.

I asked him what exactly that was about. He said he thinks I am just so different and he is attracted to me! Hmmm... I rather quickly said my goodbyes and went to get credit on my phone. I had to make an important phone call to an important person. I was not going to be a part of the after-effects of being bored out of your mind!

Notwithstanding, I will be the first to admit that Akan is actually a very likeable person and we have so much in common. He is really talented in similar ways as I am. He kept a diary like I did and wrote some really nice poems and prose. I also love the way he speaks Yoruba so well! I decided it was probably best to keep as far away as possible.

I did not feel anything special for him, but when you are thrown together in such a restricted environment, everything seems so much more intense, I think. I am a bit of a coward; so, at the slight resemblance of a chance, I am running. I do not want to lose what I have...

The rest of the day was quiet.

DAY FOURTEEN
MONDAY 200904

I did not go for drills this morning. I headed to the clinic and slept till 7:00am. I then went back to the hostels, had my bath and went back to the clinic. I am thinking of going for drills in the afternoon though, because the guys in my platoon are playing football.

The girls played volleyball this morning and they won 25-6 and 25-0. We must really be good! I was with Chizzy and Ebere. Chizzy says he has prayed to "Mother Mary" to help him get over Ebere as soon as possible. He is still hanging around her, though. We all concluded that even if the prayer has been answered, it will take a while to see the effect of it (assuming he allows it to take effect!).

Akan sent someone to call me from my room in the afternoon. I said hello and wanted to leave immediately, but thought it would not be nice, since we were not fighting. So funny how guys really do not have much respect for the fact that you already have a boyfriend. It's like, "So what?" I talked constantly about one and it did not seem to faze Akan in the slightest. The guy has raps! He deserves an award.

Once he said to me, "Let me be your nightmare if I cannot be your dreams, just let me be there please!" RAPS! How sad it was all wasted on me. He thinks I am afraid of him. I told him I am not afraid of him; I just did not like complicating my life!

We got our bicycle allowance today. It was meant to be N528, but I collected N525. Unlike me, some very thrifty people made sure they had N2 in change so they could collect all of their N528!

DAY FIFTEEN
TUESDAY 210904

Feeling like a serious Corper again today, so I got up really early and got ready for the drills. The soldiers seem to be getting tired. They did not even come back this morning apart from the little noise they made initially. My room was still full at about 5:30am when I left for the parade ground. Of course, I was mega late and so was half of my platoon. It's almost like they hand-picked all the lazy people in this batch to make up my platoon!

The Camp commandant picked on my platoon this morning. He separated those who had the proper sportswear on (white T-shirt over white shorts) from those who did not. Some of us came in jeans (I am not planning to die from the cold over the N7,500 I'm being paid by NYSC!).

The people in the correct sportswear did the marching this morning, and the rest of us just laid about a bit, after which we were allowed to sneak away for our dance rehearsals. *Indeed, soja don tire!*

Our cultural dance presentation is either tonight or tomorrow night, and in our usual "fire brigade" manner, our first proper rehearsal is this morning.

I do not have the energy for the Igbo/Urhobo dance they have chosen, therefore I am not dancing. I just sat and watched. I took some pictures in Hausa and Edo traditional costumes that did not turn out well, so I went to take another set. Akan "caught" me there and I had to take a picture with him as well (I may have promised to take a picture with him, I think).

I decided not to go back to the field for the parade. It looks like not everyone would even be marching, only about 100 people or so... that is, the best of the best from each platoon.

The Endurance Trek is on Saturday and so is Miss NYSC. There are two Corpers who are likely to represent us. it is actually supposed to be one representative per platoon, but trust my platoon to have two for them! I think we will have to vote for who finally represents us.

Our mentality that once a lady is fair-skinned she *fine* is quite interesting. Surely, I am not the only one whose got eyes that can actually see. There are lots of beautiful dark-skinned girls as well, and it is time we started to appreciate the beauty in black again.

We were immunised today against Cerebrospinal Meningitis (CSM). It happens to be endemic in Northern Nigeria and it is only right that NYSC sees that we are well-prepared to fight it. I must commend the efforts of *University of Ibadan* for taking the initiative to organise pre-camp CSM immunisation for all their students posted to the Northern parts of the country. Other institutions ought to borrow a leaf.

I generally hate needles and injections, and was very anxious about this one, but it wasn't as painful as I thought it would be. I hope the rest of the day does not prove otherwise...

Feeling very mischievous today and something tells me I need to pray extra hard to stay out of trouble. Don't worry it's not what you think...

10:00PM

I did not get in any trouble!

Meanwhile, Chizzy has always called me "Happy" from as far back as I can remember. He says he thinks I am always happy (I still cannot figure out where he got that idea from). He also says stuff like "Hi Happy." "How are you, Happy?" Well, I love the way it sounds.

Chizzy and Ebere have become very pathetic lately. They both enjoy each other's company a lot, but one thing is sure, both of them claim, they would not trade what they had before coming to Camp for this "Camp love." Chizzy has been with his girlfriend since their first year in school and Ebere has been with her boyfriend for five years now. I am not an adventurous person; better to stick with the known! I am glad they have come to that sort of conclusion...

The picture I took with Akan was ready for collection today. It turned out really nice. If anyone asks, I was coerced into taking it! Ha! Ha!

Today, I saw a guy whose mannerisms are exactly like one of my brothers. I hear he is called Dele. The semblance is so striking...

People are really sorting themselves for this one year of NYSC. They are getting up to all sorts to ensure their posting is a good one or generally trying to make sure that they can get away unnoticed...

There was plenty of drama in the clinic today; lots of raw nerves. People were shouting at each other for different reasons. There is a really haughty guy in the health team – you would think he was the only medic in the whole of Nigeria or something. I really don't like the way he carries himself. Well, I found out I am not the only one who thought that way as most other medics were not crazy about him either!

DAY SIXTEEN
WEDNESDAY 220904

Camp is getting increasingly dry. Each day is more boring than the one before and I think people are increasingly going to get up to no good as it wraps up.

I got to drills really late this morning, say about 6:30am. Of course, we did not march again in my platoon; we are all such lay-abouts! We left almost as soon as we got there. I was late for the mid-morning parade as well and got to the grounds at about 11:00am.

I got a visitor today who was sent to check on me by a friend of mine. He might be able to help work something out as per my posting, but I am not entirely comfortable with it. Somehow, I keep getting this feeling that I should "Back off!" trying to do anything clever with regards to my posting. I probably should pay attention and... back off!

Even though my platoon had not been marching for some time now, the soldiers suddenly got a brainwave this afternoon and decided to resurrect my Platoon's marching. So, I joined in. We were very few and they ended up merging us with another platoon. Dele was there, so we spoke a bit afterwards...

I had lunch and dinner with Chizzy, Ebere and Osas. Osas, Chizzy's friend, keeps saying he likes me. Unfortunately for him, I remember he was one of those fond of jumping queues during registration, which did him no favours.

Our cultural dance competition was tonight. It was so short that by the time I went to eat and came back it was over! I did not see the final showdown. I hope it was okay though. We won our third place volleyball match and won the football match, so we are in the football finals. Our guys are really good. All results will be announced tomorrow night, including dance and drama.

I spoke with the State Director today and he was so nice. I told him I was a bit apprehensive about my posting and he encouraged me to just relax and not be afraid. He said if I trusted God, everything will be fine. He even told me that his name meant "God with us," therefore no need to fear. He asked my name and when I told him, he said, "You carry God with that sort of name, there is no need to be afraid!"

I got some lovely text messages from my good friend back home, who also served in the North. I think it is almost settled in my mind; I am more likely to stay in Kano now than when I first arrived!

DAY SEVENTEEN
THURSDAY 230904

After the terrible overnight rain, the weather was chilly this morning. I decided not to go to the parade ground for morning drills. The proper Man O' War training is today. I am conserving energy for my picture taking spree! Another set of iconic NYSC pictures...

The training itself was okay... There was this bridge made with ropes, however, that I had made up my mind from the start that I was not getting on! I actually did a few of the obstacle courses, but the queues were moving rather slowly and I quickly lost interest in the rest, but not before I satisfied myself by taking pictures. How can I tell anyone I came to Camp without Man O' War pictures to show? That is a taboo!

Osas is still professing undying love for me. I told him that I am "married" to a very jealous man, but he insists he wants to take a picture with me. Unfortunately for him, I had drawn a line on picture favours. No more! It is especially difficult trying to get rid of him being Chizzy's friend. Anyway, there are just four days to go now!

We lost the final football match — to the better team, I guess. Other results are to be announced at the finals tonight, but I am not really interested in going.

One of the football players was bitten by a scorpion tonight after the match, while he was bathing. He was rushed to the clinic. We did what we could and he is better now.

Another girl had a horrid asthma attack. She started to turn blue around her lips, hands and legs. It was really scary! She was taken out of Camp because she needed oxygen and we did not have any in our "clinic." She was taken to a hospital in town and brought back not too long afterwards; they said there was no oxygen there either. Can you just imagine that? Anyway, she is now stable, but it was a scary experience.

Today, I heard someone refer to our Camp commandant as "Nightrider," because he drives this small sports car, like a *Celica* or *Prelude* (I am not good with cars so don't know for sure). He uses it to chase people around Camp without actually getting out of the car. His car alone terrorises Corpers. It is a brown car… not a nice colour, but it achieves the objective. He drives it very slowly, almost like cruising, and either uses his eyes to "speak" to Corpers to do the right thing or shouts from inside the car. It is all very menacing!

There is lots of noise from the hall as the results are being announced, but I am too tired to go anywhere. I just want to sleep!

Meanwhile, one of the *Al majiris* was said to have attempted to rape a female Corper this afternoon. She was bathing in one of the make-shift bathrooms.

God have mercy! These boys are all over the place – some trying to be useful and make a living, and others acting like you owe them money, food or some kind of favour.

DAY EIGHTEEN
FRIDAY 240904

Even with all our last-minute training and rehearsals, we still came 2nd in Football, 3rd in Volleyball, 3rd in drama and 3rd in dance. That dance? Indeed, God works in mysterious ways!

As usual, I did not go for drills this morning. I had become very lazy. Chizzy fell sick today. He needs to get out of here fast!

We are to leave for the Endurance Trek at 6:00am tomorrow, and have been strongly advised not to use creams, roll on, perfumes, powder or make-up so as not to attract bees as we go through the jungle! Hmmm, how will all those girls that make up at 5:00am cope?

We heard rumours of fighting in town. A woman was said to have torn the Koran or something like that. To think we have not even left Camp yet and this is already happening! Sometimes, I do think that people just put fuel to fire by exaggerating these stories when telling them, just to make trouble. "According to," a school teacher had come in for her lesson and some boys were reading the Koran. She asked them to put it away. When they refused, she was said to have taken it and torn it!

I would not like to believe for one minute that a sensible Nigerian who has lived in the country in the last few years would do such a thing when she knows it can cause some serious trouble. Don't people ever learn? That is why I think a lot of what we hear is exaggerated, just so the troublemakers can have a good enough reason to make trouble! It is time we really started watching our mouths and what we say, especially when we do not have first-hand information. It can do more harm than good...

We are all getting ready for the Endurance Trek. Some people are not comfortable with issues of safety, so they moved their belongings out of Camp until after the trek because we will all be gone for so long.

Akan claims he is distraught about not being able to have something he wants. I told him I could not help him. He said he did not think there was anything I could do either because I was "the problem." Really?

There was a novelty match between the Senior NYSC officials and the female Corp members. It was hilarious. It started with 16 girls (1 from each platoon) against 11 officials with the State

Director as Captain. It was quite a match as the girls were allowed to use their hands as well! There were no rules for the girls so they cheated all through, pulling T-shirts, wrestling officials to the ground. At one point, there were about ten girls trying to get the ball from one official who was on the floor! It was so funny.

As the match progressed, more girls joined in from the side lines. Soon there were about 30 girls on the field. It was pure comedy! There was even a guy who stuffed the front of his shirt like he had boobs, and walked onto the field at some point. Although it was all funny at first, it started to get really annoying when the girls started to overdo things. Well, what did I expect when there were no rules! Anyway, the officials still won 3-1 with the girls' goal coming in the second half from a penalty kick...

I am getting really homesick now and am about ready to leave this place! There is supposedly a party nearby organised for Corpers. It looks like a lot of people might have gone for it as the whole place is a bit deserted.

Well, I am off to bed early tonight. Big day tomorrow.

DAY NINETEEN
SATURDAY 250904

D-day! We woke up at about 3:30am. Of course, most of us could not imagine bathing that early in the cold, so we bathed last night. With all the rules about not using deodorants or powder or perfume, oh my… what body odour!

Breakfast was bread and "coloured water," served at about 5:00am. As I write, I still haven't eaten anything from the Camp kitchen! The only marks on my meal ticket were times I gave my ticket out to someone who had lost hers. Oddly, not eating from the Camp kitchen feels like an achievement (Ha! Ha!).

Set out time was 6:00am, but you know now, this is Nigeria after all. We did not leave until 7:00am. I met up with Yinka, another new friend, on the parade ground and stuck with her throughout.

We were asked to wear our full kit, but also advised to be as comfortable as possible. So, we were allowed to differ a bit on footwear and the T-shirts. I wore the full kit except for the crested vest because it gets really hot in that vest. Yinka arrived at camp very late, so she still does not have her kit. She wore jeans.

We walked along the main road for about 30 minutes before turning off through some foot path. We stayed in our platoons for the trek. We started out singing and feeling very jolly, but soon realised we needed to conserve our energy. People had packed food and drinks like they were going on a picnic, which turned out to be a bad idea as they were weighed down by the extra baggage.

Some Batch 'A' Corpers (those who had been serving in Kano for six months by the time we came) had advised that we go with as little as possible. I listened. I had just a bottle of water that I could sling across my body. I had bought the type that I could happily do away with. The idea was if the bottle got too heavy to carry, I would just fling it!

The business sense of Nigerians is unparalleled, I tell you. We had petty traders who actually came on the trek with us! They were selling water, *Lucozade*, sweets, biscuits etc. We even had photographers come along as well! I could not believe it. They did the journey with us just to sell their goods and services and make some money. It was good though, because without them, I probably would not have made it as I did not have breakfast. I was able to buy some *Lucozade* along the way.

Yinka also had biscuits and *Ribena*. As tempted as I was, I did not take along my Walkman. Yinka took hers and paid dearly because when she got tired, everything weighed twice as much! On the other side of the coin, however, when talking became more tasking, she was able to listen to music and I just had to do some sightseeing in the bush.

We went through a winding path, past a sugarcane plantation, then past a corn plantation, still trying hard, with little success, to remain in our platoons. We then crossed over a river. On the other side, there was a boy on a donkey. Being picture-crazy, some Corpers begged him to get off and let them take pictures with the donkey. I bet that in its entire life, that donkey had never carried as many people as it carried today. Poor donkey!

By this time, we were no longer in our lines or platoons; some people stopped practically everywhere to take pictures. As we went past a settlement, we stopped to take pictures near the huts and with the natives. It was mainly the men and children outside saying, "Sanu Nku" (which is a form of greeting in Hausa); the women only peeped from the doorways of the mud huts and didn't actually come outside.

I bet some people will spend almost N2,000 on pictures today alone because even when they coughed, they wanted a picture taken!

We then trekked on and reached another river that was completely covered by something that looked like algae. It was all green, just like a huge football field. It was beautiful and ugly at the same time. Of course, more pictures were taken here as well until the Man O' War guys came to move us along!

Some more bush… then a groundnut farm. We met farmers by the farm and some Corpers took some of their freshly harvested groundnuts and ate them raw. Yuck!

By now, we were all so tired and started asking the soldiers how much longer it was going to be. Some Corpers were talking about getting motorbikes! But because we trekked entirely through the bush, there were no cars, buses, bikes – nothing! Almost like they knew we would take the option if given!

We finally reached this place where we heard loud noises—people talking and laughing. As our little group (Yinka, myself and a few others) turned the corner, we saw a hill with Corpers at different levels, taking pictures, of course! We just looked from afar and did not go anywhere near them as we were not sure how much longer the journey was. We did not want to expend all our energy climbing the hill.

Now that I think about it, we should have just done that; we probably would not get that sort of chance again ever... at least, not to take pictures on a hill with other Corpers on an Endurance Trek at NYSC Orientation Camp! Yinka and I had simply walked on... how uninteresting!

We reached another little settlement where there was a primary school building. The Corpers were making fun of each other, saying silly things like, "This is where you will be posted; see your staff quarters..." I hope it will still be funny on Tuesday when we get our postings!

At that settlement, the women were peeping as usual, with the children outside. A male Corper wanted to take a picture beside a hut, but as he moved close to the hut, the women shouted, "Ba Shiga!" (meaning "No entry" in Hausa). The women in the hut probably thought he wanted to enter. Of course, the Corper was so scared, he ran for dear life!

My boots really started weighing me down, but I had to keep going. My water bottle was almost completely empty. The sun at 8:00am in Kano was like the midday sun anywhere else!

We heeded the advice of the elders and bought raffia hats (N20 each) as a shield against the sun. Our face caps were absolutely useless against the Kano sun!

Yinka was walking very slowly, listening to music. I did not want to walk that slow so as not to feel even more tired, so I left her behind.

We finally started hearing cars and similar noise in the distance, and I was hoping that meant something good. When we turned a corner, the Man O' War coordinator was there saying, "Well done, two minutes to first half, move it, move it!"

After a few more metres, we burst unto a main road. Just then, I hit my foot against a stone. Thank goodness, I had boots on as it really hurt, even with that. I was limping till we got to our rest spot. I stopped my timer as I walked through the gate of the school we were to rest at and waited for Yinka to catch up. Then we took our "half time" picture!

We were entertained by the OBS crew who had gone ahead to the school to set up and play music. OBS (Orientation Broadcasting Service) mostly consisted of Mass Communication students running a radio station for Camp. They acted like they were not part of the Camp. They will probably wake up and realise that they did not have the real Camp experience like the rest of us. They were always locked up in the studio whether or not they were needed there. (Actually, maybe I do not quite qualify to say this as we medics were not much different... Well, at least, I tried!).

We were given glucose and there was lots of fan milk products (for sale, of course!), water and drinks. I hear there was even rice being sold! How could I forget to add that all through the trek, I could make and receive calls. That's the kind of jungle hike I like!

The first half of our trek was 13km long, and it took about 2 hours, 35 minutes and 44 seconds. I would never have thought I could survive it, but I did. Although, my feet were almost numb by now. I sat on the floor under a tree and took my glucose, yoghurt and water.

We stayed about an hour or a little less, and started off back to Camp, but not before some people who had extra energy, God knows from where, had danced to some Camp favourites that OBS played over the speakers.

The journey back, which was along the main road, was much shorter; about 7km. It took us only 1 hour and 2 minutes. Of course, we had some "casualties;" some people jumped on a trailer that was going towards Camp; some others jumped into the ambulance. Very few people did this, actually.

I was really impressed that we had no fainting or any such thing. Someone observed that it was probably because those who could have given us the drama did not bother coming for the trek!

The journey back was uneventful. We walked about half the way with Akan. Yinka said we were dragged to victory by him because we were leaning on him, sort of! We bought some ice cream to cool off.

As we got to the gate, the Man O' War coordinator was there to congratulate us "for making it to the end of this once-in-a-lifetime opportunity" blah blah blah... Akan was more or less dragging Yinka along by this time. We went straight to the photo stand and took a victory picture! This was about 11:30am.

I went back to my room, had a bath, had some food and slept like a log of wood till about 5:00pm. I was literally dragged out of bed by one of my roommates!

I then went with Yinka to watch the Miss NYSC contest, which was sponsored by Nigerian Breweries. It was okay but truth be told, there are nicer looking girls on Camp than the ladies I saw out there! But I suppose they were the bold ones, so kudos to them. There were only seven contestants in all, and one or two that I wondered how they made it into the competition in the first place. Trust my platoon to be well represented!

There were supposed to be sixteen contestants—one from each Platoon—but there was no such luck! The contestants made an interesting mix. One was really thin; another looked like she would have fit in better in the "Mrs." NYSC competition as she just looked so much older than the rest of the girls. That is what Yoruba people will call "Aunty Agbaya!" There was yet another who acted like she'd had a strange medical condition by the way she placed her hands. It was not a good look at all! Then there was Amina from platoon seven. She did really well from the start, but her height seemed to count against her.

The contestants had to answer some questions. One of them was asked who the Governor of Kano State was and she did not know - which was quite embarrassing! I mean, not only was she serving in Kano State, we had been in Camp for almost three weeks and the Governor (or was it his deputy?) had been to Camp for the opening ceremony. Okay, let us assume this was still not sufficient reason to care who the Governor is, but if you are going in for such a competition should you not be armed with all kinds of facts, especially something as obvious as the name of the Governor?

Another contestant was asked to spell "embarrassment" and she thoroughly embarrassed herself! It was a big joke! Needless to say, Amina's height seemed not to count much against her compared with all the other flops around her. She ended up winning, not only by the judges' decision, but also by popular consensus!

There were three categories in the fashion show – white on white, traditional outfit and evening wear. No bikinis were allowed in Kano State, and when you are in Rome you've got to do what the Romans like doing, as long as it does not conflict with what you know and believe to be right (my version)! Just as well, because I really did not want to see any of that.

Joy (from my platoon) came second and the third girl had a very peculiar catwalk that I thought was cute. First prize was a microwave; second, a table top gas cooker; and third was a kettle...

Today, I showed Akan the picture I'd had in my journal, under my pillow throughout Camp. He said, "The person in the picture is worth it." Well, don't I know that already?

I slept at about 11:30pm.

DAY TWENTY
SUNDAY 260904

I woke up late and did not go for fellowship today. People are generally starting to wind down and pack their stuff together.

It was a really lazy day, except for the fact that we took room pictures, and also pictures with Amina, Miss NYSC.

I am wondering what tomorrow will be like. It has been a bitter-sweet experience for me in Camp. I liked making new friends, but absolutely hated the sanitary conditions and the early morning drills. I definitely would not want to do this again or extend my stay here. Nonetheless, it was an altogether good experience to have, I guess – rough and rugged!

Chizzy, Ebere and Osas asked me to go out with them to see someone, but I turned the offer down. I did not want to leave Camp till we had officially been asked to. I had not gone anywhere till now, so I can wait another day or two.

A bon fire night was planned for us but they say it had been banned in this part of the country. I really think we can be just a little more tolerant in this country. Why would a bon fire night be banned? Anyway, with or without any bans, people get up to all sorts anyway.

There's this "Camp couple" that caught my attention and I went "sniffing" for information. It happens that though they go everywhere together and are all over each other, the lady is supposed to be engaged and getting married in less than six months! Are they not concerned that news will travel? But they insist they are "just friends." I do think Camp is a good place to try out being faithful. Just my opinion...

Goodnight!

DAY TWENTY-ONE
MONDAY 270904

I woke up when the bugle sounded at about 4:00am. *Don't these soldiers get tired?* Anyway, they have to do it for the very last time and get their final high until the next Orientation Camp in another six months!

My bed has given way and now tilts at an awkward angle, because the khaki piece I used to tie one of its corners is now torn! I woke up with a backache and went straight to the clinic to continue sleeping. We have all become increasingly lazy, but I guess there is no point being so agile when we are not marching.

I took my bath and packed up my suitcase. My roommates were all packed up too – you'd think we were going home today! Some people had sent their stuff out of Camp already. The last day always leaves a lot of people feeling disoriented, so you need to organise yourself well beforehand.

On the last day, we all collect the letters showing our primary posting. If you are lucky, the people from your primary posting will actually come and pick you up from Camp; otherwise, you will have to find your way there. It all sounds a bit scary.

The medics are not going to collect their letters in Camp like everyone else. We are going to be taken to the Health Management Board where we would be given our postings.

I think some people already know where they are going to—good for them. But I have to wait like the rest of the masses. I only hope it all works out well. I am particularly hoping to be in the same place with someone I know, which will make life a little more bearable. I will pray and just hope for the best.

We took a group photo of the health personnel today along with Hajia, the NYSC official in charge of the Medics. There is only one physiotherapist in this batch (at least, one that we know of), Kay. He did so much work that I am sure he would have made like N500,000 if he collected N500 for each massage he did—and I am not exaggerating!

Kay lost his phone at some point in the clinic while charging it, which was really bad. It was decided that he needed to be compensated for all his hard work. So, we contributed N200 each for him to get a new handset. We raised about

N6,800 and gave it to him today. He was really grateful. I am happy we did this because it is always good to appreciate people's efforts and hard work.

I followed up on a strong impression I had to write a note to Dele. I felt strongly to tell him that God wanted him to do something in particular, and he needed to find out what it was and follow hard after it; because there is no real fulfilment outside of that. I would not normally do that with a complete stranger, but I felt so strongly about this that I wrote the note, went looking for him, handed it to him and walked away. I'm glad I did it...

We have a platoon party at 9:00pm... and being the last night in Camp, I think some people do not plan on sleeping...

I popped into the party briefly at about 9:30pm. It had not started, so I went to sleep - big day ahead tomorrow!

There is lots of partying going on around, both within and without the Mammy Market. Everybody seemed to savour the last moments of togetherness before "Almighty NYSC" flings us miles apart from our new found friends and lovers... but I honestly cannot be bothered. My bed is calling me!

DAY TWENTY-TWO
TUESDAY 280904

We needed no bugle or soldiers to wake us up today; most people were up by 3:00am! We had to submit our mattresses and get our clearance slips before 7:00am, when we needed to be on the parade ground.

I got up about 4:00am to bathe in the cold, under the full moon because I could not risk going to the "bathrooms" at that time. I got dressed in my full kit and went to submit my mattress. The principality of unruliness was at work again, and it was crazy at the hall during submission. Rather than suffocate, I gave up my space, put my mattress on the floor and lay down till the madness subsided. Afterwards, I submitted my mattress.

The parade was beautiful! The Corpers really did a brilliant job with the marching, even under the heat of the Kano midday sun.

At about 11:00am, the Camp officials started giving out the posting letters – the most effective I had seen the Camp officials since Camp started! We were all attended to within half an hour, I kid you not! It was almost like they were so glad to double their efficiency just to get rid of us! Even "Nightrider" said to us, "The Lord has delivered me from your hands today."

I got my letter and was posted to a choice hospital in town. I was really glad to be in town and not anywhere else, even though I was not sure what the place would be like.

Chizzy was flung to some village, and if I know my friend as well as I think I do, he will be finding his way back home for good shortly. Ebere got posted to the barracks and it is hard to imagine she would stay as well. Linda was also posted to a hospital in town.

I had no idea where my hospital was and I asked around. I found out it was very close by (yipee!). I then went back to the clinic to find out if there was anyone else posted there. There was someone called Brenda, who is a Medical Doctor. So, I went looking for her.

On my way to find Brenda, I saw Akan. He had been posted to some local government area about an hour away from Kano town. We said our goodbyes and he promised to call me as soon as he got a phone line that had network where he had been posted to.

Memoirs of a 'Lazy Korfa' 97

I finally found Brenda and another friend of hers, Ngozi, who was posted to a different hospital, but also in town. Brenda's husband had come to pick her up. She and her husband lived in Kano. I was so blessed to have met these girls because I was able to go with them when Brenda's husband came. He took us to the hospital and we went to report there with our letters.

We were accepted at the hospital and then asked when we wanted to resume. *Erm... just like that?* I promptly asked for a two-week break and my boss agreed and said we should come and get our acceptance letters the following day. AMAZING! This was all going so well, I thought.

We then went to eat. I had pounded yam and *Egusi* soup. It tasted great; best meal I have had in three weeks! One of my new friends, Ngozi, had already been given her own accommodation, so we all went there together. It was a nice, moderately furnished two-bedroom flat. We dropped off all our things. Brenda and her husband suggested that we could sleep over at a nearby guest house. I jumped at the opportunity. An air-conditioned room, a cozy environment, all for about N1000 sounded fantastic! But by the time we went back there, it was fully booked, thanks to the newly set-free Corpers!

I returned to the flat with Ngozi and we decided to stay there instead. It is a lovely place, although quiet. I am not sure there is a lot of work for Ngozi here at this hospital, so we have decided this is probably the year to do specialty training entry exams.

Brenda and her husband have been absolutely great, and I cannot believe how God has favoured me so much. Brenda has offered to pick me up tomorrow so we can return for our acceptance letters, and open the bank accounts we need for our allowances to be paid into. We planned to finish our clearance on Wednesday so I can go home on Thursday.

The Admin Officer at the hospital has also promised to get me my accommodation tomorrow so I can sort that out before I go and "return to a comfortable place." I'm really hoping my accommodation is good, although I am not too pleased about the way it "sounds." It is in a place called *Nomansland*, between the Barracks and Sabon Gari, where most "foreigners" in Kano reside. It is said that you almost forget you are up North when you are in Sabon Gari because everything in the South exists there... well... almost. I still have an offer from Ngozi though; she says I can stay with her if I want to. We'll have to wait and see...

I am off to bed now and absolutely grateful to God for a nice place to lay my head tonight. I called Chizzy to find out about him, Ebere and Osas. At least, he is lucky to have signal on his phone. He had what he called a 'royal welcome' in the village where he was posted to. Ha! Ha! Like a lot of other Corpers, people from the local government he was posted to came to pick them up in Camp. Electricity is not very constant there though. He says he is fine, but I hope he really is as fine as he says because he sounds pretty depressed to me.

Wow... I feel really lucky tonight.

DAY TWENTY-THREE
WEDNESDAY 290904

Brenda brought us water to bathe as we had none at Ngozi's place. We then went to get our acceptance letters, but Ngozi's was not ready. The hospital had a problem with accepting all the people that had been posted there so they were still sorting that out.

My accommodation was also not ready. I will be sharing it with another lady who is a Nurse in the hospital. I am really concerned about safety issues and hope it turns out okay.

It is sad that I would be this concerned about "safety issues" in my own country just because I do not hail from these parts and do not share the more common religion in these parts. I look forward to a time when this will be a thing of the past because if we are going to serve our country, then we deserve to feel safe wherever we are.

We went to the NYSC State Secretariat after opening our accounts at a bank where most Corpers were opening their accounts, just off

Airport Road. I wanted to make sure I did not need to spread my tentacles too wide around here and tried to keep everything within the same area as much as possible. Our Zonal Inspector was not there and we were advised to go to the Federal Secretariat. When we got there at about 4:00pm, it was already closed. Brenda then dropped us off at about 5:00pm and went home for the day.

Ngozi and I took a stroll to a nearby restaurant to have dinner later in the evening. I told her all about myself and my family. I really like her and I think I have found myself a good friend already. We have quite a lot in common and seem to think alike.

I have decided to go ahead of Brenda tomorrow because she obviously does not have the same sense of urgency that I have, to get stuff done fast and get out of here... She lives here!

DAY TWENTY-FOUR
THURSDAY 300904

I got up early and got out. My first port of call was the Airport. The idea is to get my ticket for the last flight out and leave for Lagos today, whether or not I finish the clearance.

I did not get a rebate from the airline, which did not tell too well on their ability to empathise with their customers. I would expect that even if it is N1000, there should be some rebate for Corpers who have come from so far to serve their motherland. Really, it's the least the airlines could do. But then, everyone has someone to blame; the Federal Government. The problem seems to be with the recent increase in fuel prices for the umpteenth time in the last few months; the airlines cannot break even when they don't give rebates… or so they say.

By the time I got to the hospital, Brenda was already there. So we submitted our passport photographs. I handed in my leave letter and we took breakfast to Brenda's husband on our way to the Secretariat. We got to the Secretariat and saw so many Corpers there. Nonetheless, we were attended to very quickly and did not spend up to fifteen minutes there. We will be doing no further clearance until November, I hear.

I first went to get my stuff from Ngozi's flat so I could go and see my flat before heading for the airport.

When I saw my flat, I was a little disappointed. Ngozi's offer to stay at hers is suddenly looking very appealing. The only thing is that I would not want to encroach on her privacy, and the place is really small for two people. Anyway, I cannot think about that right now. I just want to get out of here and go home. I will deal with that when I get back.

4:30PM

I am on the plane now, on my way back to Lagos for a two-week break before youth service really starts. I am not sure what to think about the adventure I have had over the last three weeks, but I am truly grateful for favour. There does not seem to be a lot of work at the hospital and I may need to help out in other departments apart from mine...

Well, here ends my three-week sojourn to a land I had never been to previously. I had heard enough to make me not want to come to Kano at all, but I am glad I came. All I can say is that God is everywhere and He rules in the affairs of men.

EPILOGUE

I was back in Kano to start my youth service two weeks after getting on that plane. I settled in quickly to life as a Youth Corp member in general, as well as working in the Hospital to which I was assigned. Over the course of the year, I pinched myself often and again — this was me not only *living* in Kano but actually *enjoying* being there. Who would have thought it? It was, in fact, one of the most enjoyable years of my life. I am so glad I did not let fear or any preconceptions get the better of me. I am delighted I made the choice not only to go to Camp, but to stay on and serve.

Although the experiences I share were a while ago; they remain some of my fondest memories. I went on to have the best one year I could have asked for in Kano and have absolutely no regrets about staying on to do my NYSC.

I met some of the most amazing people and remain good friends with many even many years on. I did lose contact with a few people immediately after Camp and was unable to get back in touch with them. However, there were people I stayed in touch with after Camp and many more that I met upon my return to start my service year.

I could certainly talk non-stop about that year. There are so many more stories to share, but that would need another book. Surely!

GLOSSARY

7/7 Kit: Refers to the 7 pieces in the complete NYSC kit including face cap, crested vest, khaki shirt, khaki trousers, belt, socks and boots.

Agbada and *Shokoto:* Traditional Nigerian outfit for men consisting of a long flowing top and trousers.

Al majiris: Usually refers to children being taught by an Islamic scholar in Northern Nigeria. They often beg for food, money and general sustenance. There were a lot of them hanging around Camp and for a small fee they often helped around with chores, like fetching water.

Aluta: Refers to 'the struggle'; usually when Corpers stand up for what they believe is their right. Sometimes involves a full on riot.

Call Up Letter: A document that shows you have been posted to a particular state for national youth service. 'Call Up Letter' because it serves as proof that you have been 'called up' to serve. Usually picked up at your University just before camp is to begin. It's like a golden ticket.

Camp commandant: The military official in charge of all the other military personnel in Camp who ran the drills and training.

Camp director: The person who was in charge of the overall running of the Camp

Camp Officials: Comprised of both civilians who were in charge of administration and the smooth running of the Camp as well as members of the Nigerian Army who were in charge of the paramilitary training we received.

Corper: Members of the National Youth Service Corps are known as Youth Corpers from which the term 'Korfa' is derived, based on the pronunciation of people from certain parts of Northern Nigeria.

Director-General: The big boss in charge of the NYSC programme across the country. May or may not be a high ranking military personnel.

Drills: Exercises and general fitness sessions.

Geles: Traditional Nigerian headgear for women.

Kit: Standard issue NYSC uniform comprising of Khaki trousers and jacket, white shorts and

T-shirts, an NYSC crested vest, a face cap, socks and a pair of boots.

Mammy Market: A make-shift market on the camp grounds where everything is sold, from food to groceries and toiletries. It was the general meeting point for Corp members and held much entertainment.

Man O' War: The paramilitary personnel who were in charge of the morning drills and other fitness training we received.

Mobilisation: A process whereby the universities send a list of eligible final year students to the NYSC national directorate who then proceed to post each student to the 36 states and the FCT as required.

Platoon: This is a subdivision of soldiers that forms a tactical unit and may also be divided into several sections. Corpers were all divided into platoons.

State director: The person who was in charge of NYSC for the entire state.

Zonal Inspector (ZI): NYSC official in charge of youth Corpers in a local government area.

KEEP IN TOUCH!

Do you have experiences and memories

of NYSC Camp and beyond?

We would love to hear from you!

Follow us on Twitter:

@lazykorfa

Follow us on Instagram:

@lazykorfa

Visit us at:

www.lazykorfa.com

Printed in Great Britain
by Amazon